GAME OF THRONES

CROSS-STITCH KIT

INSTRUCTIONS
AND

T0364037

RP Minis®
Hachette Book Group
1290 Avenue of the Americas, New York, NY 10104
www.runningpress.com
@Running_Press

First Edition: May 2024

Published by RP Minis, an imprint of Hachette Book Group, Inc. The RP Minis name and logo is a registered trademark of Hachette Book Group, Inc.

Running Press books may be purchased in bulk for business, educational, or promotional use. For more information, please contact your local bookseller or the Hachette Book Group Special Markets Department at Special.Markets@hbgusa.com.

The publisher is not responsible for websites (or their content) that are not owned by the publisher.

Patterns by Shannon Kelly
Box and interior design by Tanvi Baghele
ISBN: 978-0-7624-8695-3

CONTENTS

Cross-Stitch Basics

Cross-stitch is a wonderful craft because it's so easy to get started. You'll only need a few tools to begin. With the right fabric, a needle, embroidery floss, and a hoop, you'll be whipping up *Game of Thrones*–themed keepsakes in no time.

Supplies

◇◇◇◇◇◇◇◇◇◇◇◇◇◇◇◇◇◇◇◇◇

FABRIC

Aida cloth is made specifically for cross-stitch projects. It's comprised of tiny squares so it's easy to see where each stitch in your pattern belongs. There are three 4" x 4" pieces of 18-count (18 squares per inch) Aida cloth included in this kit to get you started. When you're in need of more, you can easily find Aida at your local craft store or online.

NEEDLES

You'll need a tapestry needle to pull your thread through the fabric. There are two included in this kit—you only need one while you work, but it doesn't hurt to have an extra on hand.

THREAD

Embroidery floss is a type of thread with six strands twisted together, and it's especially well-suited to cross-stitch. This kit includes four skeins in the colors you'll need to complete any of the patterns in this book: black, gray, red, and gold.

HOOP

An embroidery hoop keeps your fabric taut as you work. Included in your kit is a 3-inch plastic hoop. You can either remove the pattern from the hoop after you're finished and frame it or leave your finished piece in the hoop to display. Simply gather the excess cloth to the back of your hoop, snip off the corners, and sew a running stitch around it to keep it out of view.

Stitching

PREPARING

First, load your fabric into your hoop. Unscrew the tightening device at the top of your hoop until it's loose enough that you can remove the inner ring. Center your cloth on the inner ring and place the outer hoop over the top, sandwiching the cloth between the two hoops. Press down so the outer ring covers the inner ring completely and tighten the screw until the fabric is taut and smooth.

Next, thread your needle. Select the color of thread that corresponds to the stitches in the center of your pattern (more on that in a moment) and cut a piece roughly 18 inches long. Separate two of the six strands and feed those two strands through the eye of your needle. Don't knot the thread.

CROSS-STITCHING

One of the easiest ways to start is by moving from the center of the pattern outward. The patterns in this book use the counted cross-stitch method (rather than a design printed on the fabric), so you'll count the number of stitches in the color you're using and then make those stitches on your fabric.

Making Single Stitches

1. Beginning at the center of the pattern (or wherever you'd like to start), pull your thread up through the hole at the **bottom left** corner of your first square. Leave a 1-inch tail of floss on the underside of the fabric. Hold on to that tail as you make your next few stitches over it—you'll want the back side of your stitches to cover the tail, which will secure it in place without a lumpy knot.

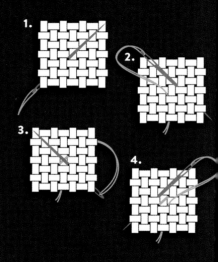

2. Insert your needle back down through the **top right** corner of the same square, creating a diagonal line on the front of the fabric. Bring your thread through to the back, taking care not to pull it too tightly—the goal is a smooth surface without any puckering. This is the first half of your stitch.

3. Bring your needle back up to the front through the **bottom right** corner of the square.

4. Pull your thread fairly taut and cross the square diagonally, inserting your needle down through the **top left** hole. This will complete the x shape of your cross-stitch.

5. To continue, bring your needle up through the **bottom left** corner of the square you want to stitch next.

Making a Row of Stitches

1.

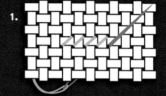

2.

1. To work a row in the same color, create the first half of each of the stitches by repeating steps 1 and 2 from the previous list over and over, moving from left to right until you've created a row of diagonal lines all going from bottom left to top right.

2. When you reach the end of the row, bring your needle up through the bottom right hole and work your way back across, completing the *x* shape of each square as you go.

BACKSTITCHING

Backstitching is a great way to add details and outlines to your patterns, especially at this miniature size. For backstitching, you don't need to work in crosses in the grid pattern of the Aida cloth—this method is more like typical embroidery than cross-stitch.

To start your backstitch, thread your needle with **two** strands of thread, and this time, make a double knot at the end of your floss, leaving a ½-inch tail at the end. Then, find the area where you want your detail line to begin and push your needle up through the back of the fabric at that point. Pull the thread through to the front and insert the needle back into the fabric to create a line segment. Continue stitching forward on the underside

and doubling back on the top surface to create more line segments
wherever the pattern calls for it. To
finish, use your needle to work your
thread through a few stitches on
the underside to secure its tail, then
snip off the excess.

PATTERNS

■ DMC 310   ■ DMC 304

■ DMC 310	■ DMC 304
▨ DMC 680	■ DMC 169

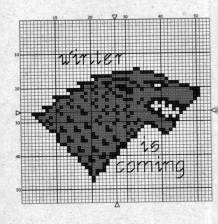

■ DMC 310   ■ DMC 169

I drink
& I
know
things

■ DMC 310   ■ DMC 304
■ DMC 680   ■ DMC 169

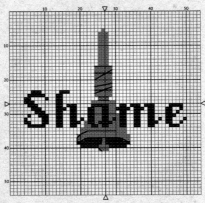

■ DMC 310 ■ DMC 169
■ DMC 680